Our Planet's Most Endangered Birds

A Product of Kesem Books LLC.

For questions contact us at:
contact@kesembooks.com

"Time is running out for countless species.
Their fate is in our hands." - Unknown

www.SavingEndangeredSpecies.org

THANK YOU

Thank you for choosing our book! Scan the code below to unlock your **FREE thank-you gift:** "Endangered Species Kids Activity Pack."

Your support means the world to us as we passionately strive to raise awareness to saving endangered species. We firmly believe that education and knowledge are the vital first steps.

We hope you enjoy this book, please consider leaving a review on Amazon; your feedback supports us and helps others discover our book.

THIS BOOK BELONGS TO:

____

____

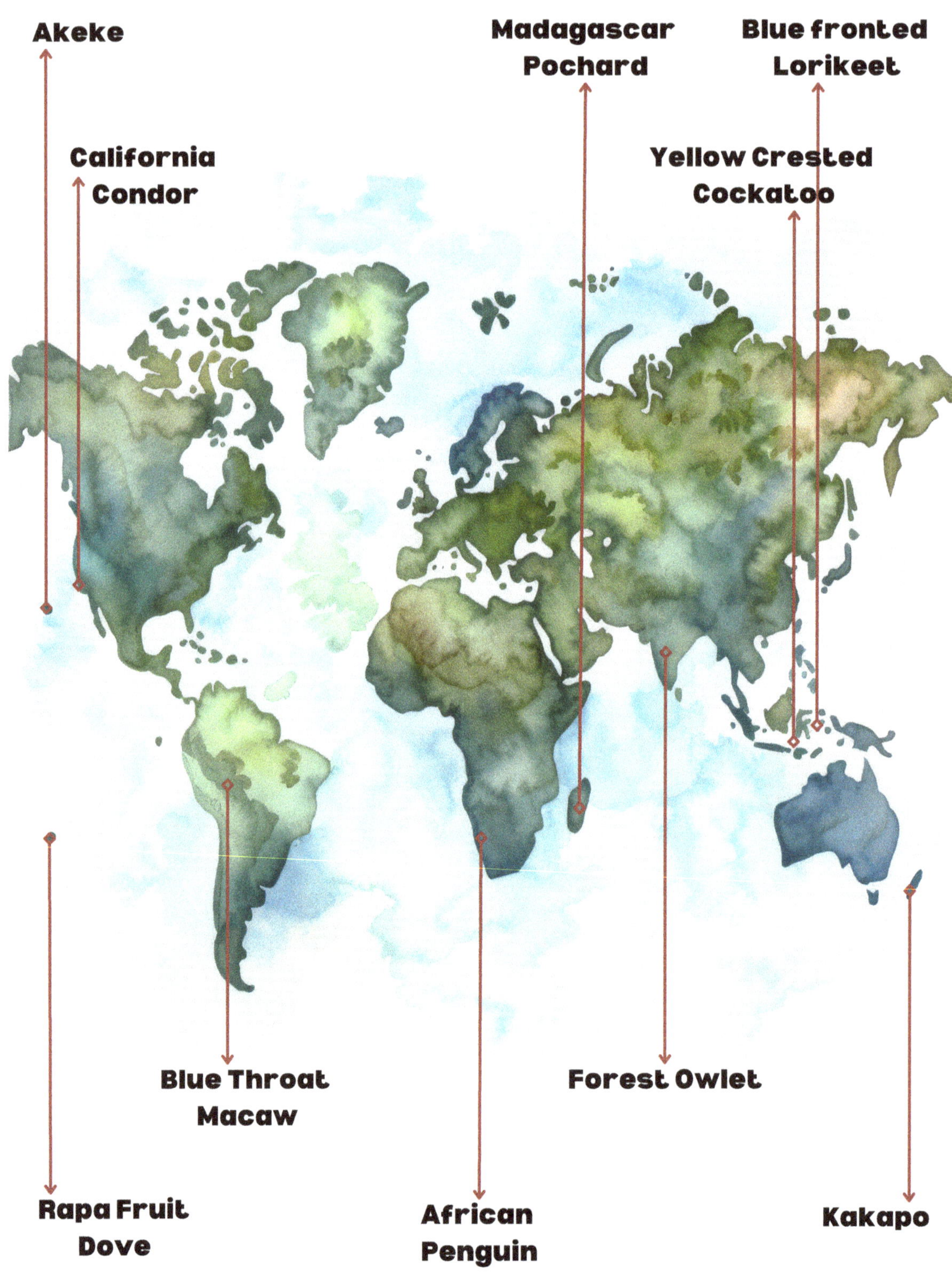

Akeke
California Condor
Madagascar Pochard
Blue fronted Lorikeet
Yellow Crested Cockatoo
Blue Throat Macaw
Forest Owlet
Rapa Fruit Dove
African Penguin
Kakapo

TABLE OF CONTENTS

DON'T LET THEM

DISAPPEAR

INTRODUCTION

Incredible birds inhabit our planet, soaring through the high skies, nesting in lush tropical rainforests, and diving into icy waters. Each bird is unique with fantastic adaptations.

Unfortunately, a growing number of these extraordinary birds face the serious threat of extinction. Shockingly, one out of every eight bird species is endangered.

Humans, with all their amazing abilities, have unintentionally created a significant impact on the world and its wildlife. This impact includes habitat destruction, invasive species, pet trading, overfishing, and many more detrimental actions.

However, humans' actions can also become the solution to ensure the survival of these remarkable creatures. Conservationists are working tirelessly worldwide! Their efforts encompass habitat protection, captive breeding programs, and public awareness campaigns, all of which are crucial for saving endangered birds and maintaining the biodiversity and balance of ecosystems on our planet. From success stories to ongoing battles, their efforts aim to secure a bright future for our endangered feathered friends. We hold the power to make a difference!

What are Endangered Species?

Endangered species include Birds, Mammals, Fish, Amphibians and Plants, that are at risk of becoming extinct and disappearing from our world forever.

Worldwide there are more than 42,100 species that are threatened with extinction, which are almost a third of all the assessed species.

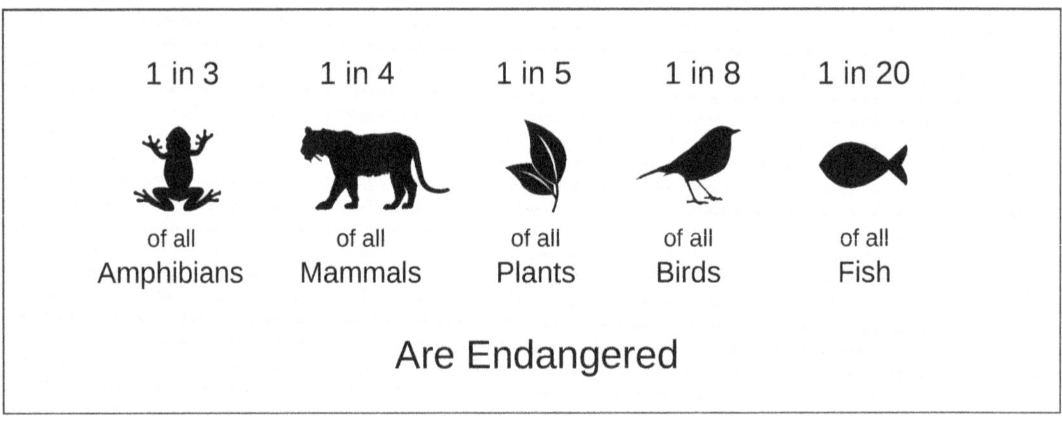

In this book we will focus on Endangered Birds. Currently, 1 out of every 8 bird species is Endangered. Therefore, 1 out of every 8 bird species is in risk of extinction through all or through most of its habitat range.

Once a species goes extinct, it is gone forever, and there is no going back.

Endangered species share several characteristics that make them vulnerable to extinction:

First, they often have a small population, which makes them susceptible to environmental changes & genetic problems.

Second, they have a limited geographic range, which means they only live in a small area, making them vulnerable to habitat loss and other threats in their living area.

Third, they often have specialized habitat requirements, which means they need a specific type of environment to survive, making them even more vulnerable to habitat loss and degradation.

Fourth, they often have low reproductive rates, which means they have fewer offspring and take longer to recover from population declines.

Finally, they are often threatened by human activities such as habitat destruction, pollution, and over-harvesting.

Why Are Bird Species Endangered?

Several factors contribute to the endangerment of bird species worldwide. Here are the main ones:

Loss of Habitat: Millions of acres of bird habitat are lost or degraded every year. The clearing of forests for timber, agriculture, or urban development destroys vital habitats for birds and other animals. This loss of habitat disrupts the natural ecosystems that birds rely on for nesting, foraging, and breeding, leading to population declines and increased vulnerability to other threats.

Human-caused Mortality: Collisions with structures such as buildings and power lines cause numerous bird fatalities each year, significantly impacting bird populations.

Hunting and Illegal Trade:
Despite legal protections, some bird species are still being hunted for food, for sport, or for the illegal pet trade, leading to population declines and local extinctions.

Climate Change: The rapid warming of the planet has caused habitat disruption, changing the availability of suitable habitats for birds and affecting their breeding and feeding grounds. For example, changes in food availability impact bird species and require them to adapt. Changes in temperature patterns can disrupt the timing of birds' key life cycle events, such as migration and breeding, leading to mismatches with essential resources.

Invasive Species and Disease Outbreaks:
The introduction of non-native species has disrupted ecosystems and posed a significant threat to many bird species, particularly those with limited distribution, such as island species. Invasive species can outcompete native birds for resources or directly prey on them, while disease outbreaks can cause significant mortality in bird populations.

Pollution: Air, water, and soil pollution, including lead poisoning and chemical contamination, are all harmful and affecting bird populations, leading to impaired health and increased mortality.

Who Are the Endangered Birds?

The status of the different species is determined by various organizations, including the International Union for Conservation of Nature (IUCN), which maintains the **Red List of Threatened Species**.

The Red List defines the severity and specific causes of a species' threat of extinction and has seven levels of conservation: least concern, near threatened, vulnerable, endangered, critically endangered, extinct in the wild, and extinct.

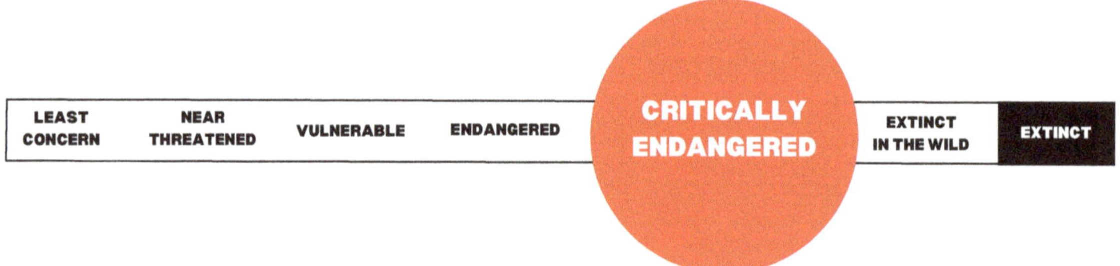

The classification of a species as endangered has to do with its range and habitat, as well as its actual population. For this reason, a species can be of least concern in one area and endangered in another.

The most endangered species on our planet are those that are classified as critically endangered, which means they face an extremely high risk of extinction in the wild, in all areas.

To determine the absolute "most" endangered species, you would need to consider factors such as the size of the remaining population, the rate of decline, the extent of their habitat loss, and the severity of threats they face. These factors can change over time, and new assessments are regularly made by conservation organizations and experts to determine the current status of various species.

In this book we will focus on ten examples of critically endangered birds. Unfortunately, there are many more endangered birds facing critical threats. Conservation efforts are needed to protect all threatened species, it is up to us to take action to protect them.

KĀKĀPŌ

The kākāpō is one of the rarest and most endangered parrots in the world with only around 200 remaining in the wild, bringing them close to extinction.

Native to New Zealand, the kākāpō is a unique parrot species, known for its impressive size, nocturnal habits, inability to fly, and a distinctive owl-like face.

The main threat to the kākāpō's survival is **habitat loss** due to forest clearance. Another significant challenge comes from **invasive species**. When European settlers reached New Zealand, they brought animals like cats, rats, ferrets, and stoats, posing a serious threat to adult kākāpō, their eggs, and chicks, and also competing with them for food and resources. As a result, the kākāpō population faced a rapid decline.

Moreover, **over-hunting** by humans has played a significant role in their decreasing numbers, pushing these unique parrots close to extinction.

Conservation efforts, such as relocating kākāpō to predator-free islands and closely monitoring them, are making a difference, gradually increasing their numbers. Conservation programs are actively working to safeguard and boost the population of these exceptional birds, with the ultimate goal of returning them to their original home by 2050.

LEAST
CONCERN
NEAR
THREATENED
VULNERABLE
ENDANGERED
CRITICALLY
ENDANGERED
EXTINCT
IN THE WILD
EXTINCT

AFRICAN PENGUIN

The African penguin is the only penguin species found in Africa, mainly on islands off the coasts of Namibia and South Africa. Today, their population is estimated at fewer than 11,000 breeding pairs, compared to millions in the beginning of the 20th century, and their numbers keep going down.

A combination of threats has led to the drastic decline in their populations, here are a few of the threats they face:

Overfishing: The big fishing operations have caused a drop in the number of sardines and anchovies, which are crucial foods for African penguins. Therefore it is harder for the penguins to get enough food, they swim farther, find less nutritious prey and are forced to leave their chicks behind for longer.

Climate Change and Ocean Warming: The changing climate and warmer oceans mean less prey for the penguins, making it even tougher for them to find food to survive and reproduce.

Water Pollution: The busy shipping lanes near South Africa are a big problem. In 2000, a huge oil spill affected 40 percent of the penguin population.

Habitat Destruction: Losing places to breed along the Namibian and South African coastlines has seriously hurt the species.

LEAST
CONCERN
VULNERABLE
ENDANGERED
CRITICALLY
ENDANGERED
EXTINCT
IN THE WILD
EXTINCT

YELLOW CRESTED COCKATOO

The wild population of the yellow-crested cockatoo is estimated to range between 1,000 and 2,500 individuals. These numbers continue to decline, posing a high risk of extinction.

The Yellow-crested cockatoos can be found on the islands of Indonesia. Variety of threats contribute to their status:

Illegal Trapping: These birds are highly valued in the illegal pet trade, where they are bought for high prices, sometimes exceeding the average annual income in Indonesia. The demand for these birds as pets has led to unsustainable trapping from the wild. Despite legal protections, loopholes in regulations and challenges in enforcement allow for continued illegal trade of these birds.

Habitat Loss: Destruction of its natural habitat through logging, deforestation, and conversion of primary forests for agriculture has drastically reduced available living and breeding areas for the yellow-crested cockatoo. This loss of habitat makes it increasingly challenging for the species to find suitable places to thrive and reproduce, creating competition with other birds for nest sites.

Low Reproductive Rate: Cockatoos have long-lived and monogamous pairs that do not start breeding until they are at least six years old. This slow rate of reproduction makes it difficult for the population to recover from declines.

LEAST CONCERN
NEAR THREATENED
VULNERABLE
ENDANGERED
CRITICALLY ENDANGERED
EXTINCT IN THE WILD
EXTINCT

AKEKE

The 'Akeke'e has experienced a population decline of 98% over the last 25 years, and is currently listed as critical endangered status, with an estimate of only 638 individuals remaining.

This species can be found only on the Hawaiian island of Kaua'i, predominantly inhabiting high-elevation forests that remain almost untouched.

A main threat to the 'Akeke'e includes a **disease**, a mosquito-borne avian malaria. **Climate change** makes this threat even worse by facilitating the spread of mosquitoes to higher elevations, posing a significant risk to the remaining wild populations.

With its specialized bill, the 'Akeke'e adeptly pries open buds of 'ōhi'a leaves and flowers in search of invertebrates.

Invasive species like yellow-jackets wasps and ants compete over these same resources. Invasive species like rats, cats, and owls add predator pressure threat. In addition, the spread of non-native plants creates **habitat degradation** and reduces suitable habitats for the Akeke'e.

Invasive mammals, such as goats and pigs alter the natural landscape which disrupts the natural water flow, creating stagnant water sources. These water pools are ideal for mosquito breeding, increasing the mosquito avian malaria disease risk for the Akeke.

#

LEAST CONCERN
NEAR THREATENED
VULNERABLE
ENDANGERED
CRITICALLY ENDANGERED
EXTINCT IN THE WILD
EXTINCT

FOREST OWLET

The forest owlet, a critically endangered bird, found in the forests of central India, with a population ranging from a mere 50 to just 400 individuals.

Once believed to be extinct, the forest owlet made a surprising comeback in 1997, but it's still classified as Critically Endangered. The survival of this remarkable bird is under threat due to severe **habitat loss** caused by deforestation, logging, agriculture, plantations, and wood gathering. This has confined the species to isolated populations within patches of forests covering less than 7 square kilometers.

The remaining **habitat is fragmented** and isolated, making the forest owlet highly vulnerable to further population decline and potential extinction. On top of that, the bird faces threats from changes in climate, hunting, predator attacks, and nest failure due to habitat loss. The fact that the bird is active during the day adds an extra layer of vulnerability to these threats.

Conservation efforts are underway to protect the forest owlet, including the creation of forest reserves and strict regulations on human activities and hunting within its habitat. These measures aim to ensure the survival of this extraordinary bird.

LEAST CONCERN
NEAR THREATENED
VULNERABLE
ENDA
CRITICALLY ENDANGERED
EXTINCT IN THE WILD
EXTINCT

23

CALIFORNIA CONDOR

The California condor, North America's largest flying bird with a wingspan of up to 10 feet (3 meters), is critically endangered, with only around 300 remaining in the wild.

The California condor faces several threats in the wild. The most significant threat is **lead poisoning**, primarily from the ingestion of lead ammunition fragments left in animal carcasses. Other threats include **micro trash ingestion, power line electrocution, habitat destruction** for example **by oil and gas drilling**.

In the 1980s, the California Condor population dwindled to just 27 individuals left in the wild, prompting collaborative conservation efforts led by the U.S. Fish and Wildlife Service and partners. Conservation strategies were developed to address the various threats and ensure the recovery of the California condor population.

A successful captive breeding program has contributed to a steady population increase. As of 2023, over 500 condors exist, with about 300 in the wild. These efforts offer hope for the species' survival, but ongoing vigilance and conservation actions are crucial to secure a sustainable future for the majestic California condor.

LEAST CONCERN
NEAR THREATENED
ENDANGERED
CRITICALLY ENDANGERED
EXTINCT IN THE WILD
EXTINCT

BLUE THROAT MACAW

The blue-throated macaw is the rarest macaw species in the world, with an estimated 350-400 individuals left in the wild, they are critically endangered.

The blue-throated macaw are found in northern Bolivia, their habitat surrounding the major city of Trinidad. As the city has expanded, the bird's numbers have declined. A main threat is **Habitat loss**, trees are cut down for firewood, building materials, and sometimes burned to improve grazing grass quality. This loss of mature trees, particularly motacú palms preferred by the macaws for nesting, forces them to compete with other bird species like toucans for limited nesting cavities.

Historically, **poaching** for the global pet trade posed a significant threat. However, conservation efforts and legislation such as the U.S. Wild Bird Conservation Act and Europe's ban on the import of wild birds have helped reduce this threat.

Additionally, the species faces threats from **climate change**, which brings about increased storms and flooding in their range.

To safeguard this species from extinction, there are ongoing conservation efforts include the creation of protected areas, planting trees for habitat restoration and installing nest boxes to enhance breeding success.

LEAST CONCERN
NEAR THREATENED
VULNERABLE
ENDANGERED
CRITICALLY ENDANGERED
EXTINCT IN THE WILD
EXTINCT

MADAGASCAR POCHARD

The Madagascar pochard, is the rarest duck on our planet, with only about 33-47 mature individuals remaining in the wild.

This Critical Endangered species is the only pochard in the western Indian Ocean. It was once relatively widespread, but severe environmental degradation in Madagascar led to its decline.

The main threats include **habitat loss** due to deforestation and wetland conversion for agriculture. **Hunting** - the pochard is hunted and trapped for food, contributing to its decline. **By-catch from fishing -** Accidental capture in fishing nets (by-catch) poses a threat to the pochard population. **Invasive species** - Introduction of non-native species like Tilapia fish into various lakes in Madagascar for farming purpose, has had a detrimental impact on the pochard. The Tilapia disrupt the ecosystem, making it difficult for the pochards to find food.

Conservation breeding plays a crucial role in the efforts to save the Madagascar pochard. Their efforts have successfully established over 100 pochards thriving in captivity. Finding a suitable habitat for releasing them back into the wild is crucial, highlighting the importance of collaborative conservation strategies in protecting these endangered species and their habitats.

LEAST CONCERN
NEAR THREATENED
VULNERABLE
ENDANGERED
CRITICALLY ENDANGERED
EXTINCT IN THE WILD
EXTINCT

RAPA FRUIT DOVE

The Rapa fruit dove is found only on the island of Rapa Iti in French Polynesia. The population is very small, estimated to be around 270 individuals, and surveys suggest that it's even getting smaller.

This bird's natural home is the small area of tropical lowland forests on the island of Rapa Iti. Unfortunately, this forest habitat is being destroyed and **Habitat loss** is the primary reason for the decreasing population size of the Rapa fruit dove. Sadly, today there is hardly any of the island's original native forests left. The destruction of the forests is caused by logging, fires, and the increased need for land for cattle and goats for grazing.

The quality of the remaining forest habitat has also been reduced due to invasive species, further decreasing the availability of suitable living and breeding areas for the Rapa fruit dove. **Invasive species**, such as goats, rats, and feral cats, pose significant threats to the plants and animals native to Rapa Iti. Goats consume native plants, while rats and feral cats attack chicks and eggs.

The combined impact of these invasive species has made it increasingly challenging for the Rapa fruit dove to find suitable places to live and reproduce posing a serious threat to its survival.

LEAST
CONCERN
NEAR
THREATENED
VULNERABLE
ENDANGERED
CRITICALLY
ENDANGERED
EXTINCT
IN THE WILD
EXTINCT

BLUE-FRONTED LORIKEET

The Blue-fronted Lorikeet is a parrot endemic to the Indonesian island of Buru. It is critically endangered, with a population size of 50-249 mature individuals.

The Blue-fronted Lorikeet primarily feeds on nectar and pollen from flowering trees. The clearing of forests for **logging** purposes impacts the availability of flowering trees and directly affects the lorikeet's ability to find food. Additionally, these logging activities have detrimental effects on the lorikeet population, causing **habitat loss** and fragmentation, destruction of nesting sites and disrupting the lorikeet's breeding and foraging behaviors.

The increase in storm activity due to **climate change** poses another threat to the lorikeet population. Severe storms impact and destruct the lorikeets' habitat, reducing available nesting sites and leading to population declines.

Another main threat is created by the introduction and establishment of **invasive species**, such as rats, cats, and Swamp Harriers (birds of prey native to Australia and New Zealand), which pose a direct threat to the lorikeet population by preying on the lorikeets and their eggs. These invasive species lead to increased predator pressure, resulting in reduced breeding success and population decline for the lorikeets.

LEAST
CONCERN
NEAR
THREATENED
VULNERABLE
ENDANGERED
CRITICALLY
ENDANGERED
EXTINCT
IN THE WILD
EXTINCT

How Can We Help?

There are many ways that you can help protect endangered birds and their habitats. Remember that every small action contributes to a significant difference, and your efforts can play a crucial role in preserving our planets diverse birdlife.

Here are some things you can do to make a difference:

Learn about endangered birds in your area:
Educate yourself about endangered birds in your region, understanding the threats and challenges they face. Share this knowledge with your friends and family, spreading awareness about the importance of protecting these fascinating species and their habitats.
Organize birdwatching adventures to observe and learn about different bird species in their natural habitats, discovering their significance in the ecosystem.

Advocate for stronger environmental policies:

Write letters to your local newspaper or elected officials, urging measures that protect endangered birds and their habitats from threats like habitat destruction, pollution, and over-harvesting.

Your voice can be a powerful force in ensuring the protection of endangered birds and their habitats.

Reduce, Reuse, Recycle:

Decrease your reliance on single-use plastics, actively, engage in recycling, and embrace composting.

These eco-friendly practices contribute to minimizing pollution and safeguarding crucial bird habitats. Your efforts in reducing environmental impact play a vital role in creating a safer and healthier environment for birds.

Don't litter or destroy sensitive bird habitats:

Help protect endangered species by not littering or destroying sensitive habitats, which may be home to native or migrating bird species that are endangered or threatened. Organize or participate in a "clean up" campaign of an important habitat in your area.

Plant a Bird-Friendly Garden:

Create a bird friendly space in your backyard by planting native plants that attract birds, offering them natural food and shelter. This creates a welcoming habitat for birds and contributes to their overall well-being.

Hang a Bird Feeder:

Install a bird feeder in your yard and keep it stocked with bird-friendly food. This provides a vital food source for local bird populations, especially during challenging times such as winter or migration.

Support bird conservation organizations:

This is a great way to make a difference!

There are numerous organizations that work tirelessly to help birds worldwide. You can volunteer your time, organize fundraisers, or donate to support their crucial work. Their efforts can be categorized into four main areas:

Firstly, <u>habitat conservation</u> is essential for bird survival. This involves preserving and restoring natural habitats, including protected areas like national parks and wildlife reserves.

Secondly, <u>captive breeding and reintroduction programs</u> are vital for critically endangered bird species. These programs help maintain genetic diversity and prevent extinction. Once populations are healthy enough, individuals are reintroduced into their natural habitats to boost wild populations.

Thirdly, <u>conservation efforts target specific threats</u> to birds, such as human activities. This includes implementing regulations on hunting and trade, creating bird-friendly infrastructure to prevent collisions, and controlling the spread of invasive species.

Lastly, <u>raising public awareness and education</u> about bird conservation is crucial. Education programs engage local communities, policymakers, and stakeholders to gather support for bird protection initiatives.

Find the organization and activity with which you resonate and join the effort!

LEARN MORE & BOOK RESOURCES

There are countless books and websites where you can discover a wealth of knowledge about Endangered Species. We highly recommend beginning your journey with the following resources, which have also been instrumental in shaping this book:

Abcbirds
Animal Fact Guide
Animaliaa
Avibase - The World Bird Database
Bird Life International
Birds of the World
Center for Biological Diversity
Cockatoo Sanctuary
Earth.com
Kauai Forest Bird Recovery Project
National Geographic
National Park Service
New Zealand Birds Online
Sanccob Saves Seabirds
Synchronicity Earth
U.S. Fish & Wildlife Service
World Parrot Trust
World Wildlife Fund

MORE BOOKS TO ENJOY

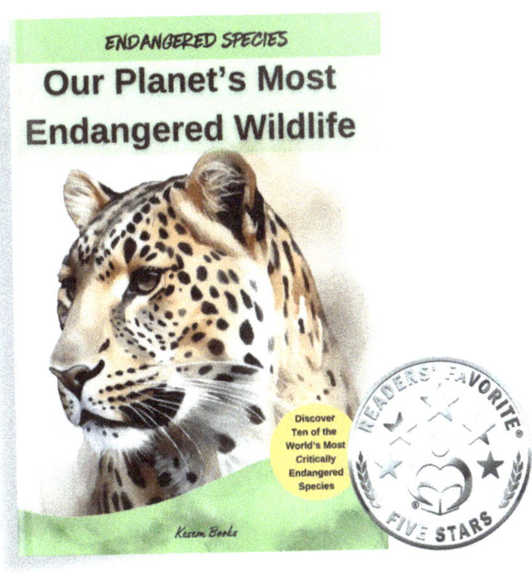

To learn more about endangered species visit our website:
www.SavingEndangeredSpecies.org